Boys and Girls
Around the World

Kelly Doudna

Consulting Editor, Diane Craig, M.A./Reading Specialist

ABDO
Publishing Company

Published by ABDO Publishing Company, 4940 Viking Drive, Edina, Minnesota 55435.

Printed in the United States.

Credits
Edited by: Pam Price
Curriculum Coordinator: Nancy Tuminelly
Cover and Interior Design and Production: Mighty Media
Photo Credits: BananaStock Ltd., Corbis Images, PhotoDisc

Library of Congress Cataloging-in-Publication Data

Doudna, Kelly, 1963-
      Boys and girls around the world / Kelly Doudna.
         p. cm. -- (Around the world)
      Includes index.
      Summary: Describes how boys and girls are treated around the world.
      ISBN 1-59197-564-6
       1. Boys--Social conditions--Juvenile literature. 2. Girls--Social conditions--Juvenile literature. [1. Culture.] I. Title.

HQ775.D68 2004
305.23--dc22
                                                                    2003058398

SandCastle™ books are created by a professional team of educators, reading specialists, and content developers around five essential components that include phonemic awareness, phonics, vocabulary, text comprehension, and fluency. All books are written, reviewed, and leveled for guided reading, early intervention reading, and Accelerated Reader® programs and designed for use in shared, guided, and independent reading and writing activities to support a balanced approach to literacy instruction.

Let Us Know

After reading the book, SandCastle would like you to tell us your stories about reading. What is your favorite page? Was there something hard that you needed help with? Share the ups and downs of learning to read. We want to hear from you! To get posted on the ABDO Publishing Company Web site, send us e-mail at:

sandcastle@abdopub.com

SandCastle Level: Fluent

Boys and girls around the world are treated differently.

Understanding and accepting these differences is important.

It makes the world a more peaceful place to live.

Trish and Mark live
in the United States.

They both go to
school five days
a week.

Ali lives in Tanzania.

He attends class while his sister works.

Girls do not go to school in many countries.

Tammy lives in England.

Her parents say it is okay to go out with her friends.

Dolie lives in Somalia.

She cannot go out
in public without a
parent or brother.

Pam lives in New Zealand.

She goes to the store by herself.

Maya, Lili, and their brothers live in Malaysia.

Some girls must be covered from head to toe when they leave the house.

Are boys and girls treated differently where you live?

Did You Know?

More boys than girls are born in the world.

There are 130 million children around the world who do not go to primary school. Two-thirds of these children are girls.

In the United States, one-third of boys and girls aged 6–11 play soccer.

In Japan there is a festival called *Shichi-go-san*, or 7-5-3. It is only for girls ages 3 and 7 and boys ages 3 and 5.

Glossary

accept. to think of as normal, right, or unavoidable

attend. to be present at

cover. to place something on or over

different. not alike

peaceful. calm, free from disagreement

public. a place visible to all people in the community

store. a place where things are sold

understand. to know well due to close contact and experience

world. the planet Earth

About SandCastle™

A professional team of educators, reading specialists, and content developers created the SandCastle™ series to support young readers as they develop reading skills and strategies and increase their general knowledge. The SandCastle™ series has four levels that correspond to early literacy development in young children. The levels are provided to help teachers and parents select the appropriate books for young readers.

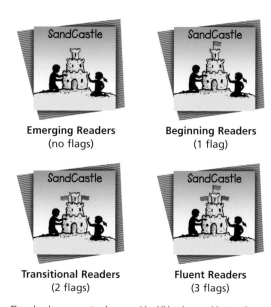

Emerging Readers
(no flags)

Beginning Readers
(1 flag)

Transitional Readers
(2 flags)

Fluent Readers
(3 flags)

These levels are meant only as a guide. All levels are subject to change.

To see a complete list of SandCastle™ books and other nonfiction titles from ABDO Publishing Company, visit www.abdopub.com or contact us at:

4940 Viking Drive, Edina, Minnesota 55435 • 1-800-800-1312 • fax: 1-952-831-1632